Perk Your Sphere

Perk Your Sphere

How To Reward Those Who Reward You

Written by Liz Johnson, Edited by Lora Ackermann,
Forward by Ande Dunn

ISBN-13: **9781540755193**
ISBN-10: **1540755193**
Library of Congress Control Number: **2016920184**
CreateSpace Independent Publishing Platform
North Charleston, South Carolina

This book is dedicated first and foremost to my son, Dane. He inspires me to be a better person in all that I do, and it is because of him that I work as hard as I do so that I can leave a legacy for him. This book is also dedicated to my clientele, who continue to refer me business year after year, and for that, I am eternally grateful.

Contents

Acknowledgments

Where do I begin? Let's see...I'll start at the beginning! First acknowledgment goes to my former Mega Achievement Productivity Systems (MAPS) coach, Dru Lee, who painfully pointed out that I was getting a terrible rate of return out of my database when it came to referrals. Dru is the one who told me I needed to find a way to reconnect with my past clients to ensure that I didn't lose touch with them.

Next I'd like to acknowledge Jeremy Mellick, a friend, colleague, and sometime competitor. He told me about his system right around the time that Dru told me to figure something out, and I modified Jeremy's system in a way that would work for me and my budget.

Now let me acknowledge Ashley Lunn, my current MAPS coach. Ashley is the one who discovered I was getting a seventeen-to-one rate of return on this program and encouraged me to write it all out and publish a book about it. Without Ashley pushing me to do this, you would not be reading this book!

Lastly and definitely NOT least, let me give huge acknowledgements to Ande Dunn, my executive assistant, who helped me write this book and bring this whole project to fruition. Without Ande, there would be no execution here, just a great idea that I was implementing.

Foreword

by Ande Dunn, Executive Assistant
The REEA: Behind the Scenes

"Coming *from the heart of a teacher"* is a commonly heard phrase around the Keller Williams's real estate office. I think that you will find Liz Johnson exemplifies this in her new book, *Perk Your Sphere*.

This book is written from the heart, and it is the result of the struggles and triumphs of someone who has actually used this program. She encourages you to grow your business and learn from her mistakes along the way.

The approach Liz offers in this book is a system literally *anyone* can follow. She laid out a plan, followed it, and has been enjoying the fruits of her labor for years. She now shares her program so others can prosper in ways they may not have thought possible.

As Einstein said, *"No thought is original."* While there have been others who have used similar programs, no one else has written about and shared his or her program in the way Liz lays it out here for you.

For the millions of real estate agents who want to build success-ful and sustained businesses, *Perk Your Sphere* is absolutely a guide on how to do that. When you see how easy it truly is, you'd be crazy not to implement it in your own business. Whether you're a brand new agent or a seasoned professional, this plan this can grow any business.

Liz has taken the referral business model, blended it with the theory of exponential growth, and has put them together to create a simple, user-friendly program.

Save yourself the heartache of how to build an effective and steady referral business and follow the steps Liz has laid out for you.

Watching firsthand how Liz's business has grown as a result of her utilization of this program has been an eye-opening experience. How can a broker be so successful *without making a single cold call* in over a year? If you're looking to up your game, you have found just the thing to take your real estate career to the next level.

Introduction

Hi! My name is Liz Johnson, and I hate cold calling. Okay, maybe hate is too strong a word, but I *strongly dislike* cold calling.

Unlike a business model that is dependent on cold calling, the business model I want to share with you is about building relationships.

The advice I'm going to divulge to you in this book could be a **game changer** for you, and it will transform the way you do business if you follow the plan. I know. I know. Every book says that. *"This is going to change your life! In six easy steps!"* While I can't say for certain that this book is going to change your life (in six or fewer steps), I *can* say that the program I outline is a different way of thinking about how you interact with your clients and your community. Who knows, it *might* even change your life. The steps to making this program work are all here in this book; read it in its entirety before you jump in.

Trust me—it's not that long of a read, and the rewards of this program may last the rest of your career.

The most important part of this program is to shift your focus from chasing stale leads to focusing on your clients—both past and present. You're going to learn how to make your clients feel special.

Though they don't have to, the clients whom you can get to feel this way will end up doing some of your legwork for you. Keep reading; you'll see what I mean.

Why this? Why not stick to just e-mailing your clients about the real estate market once a month, sending a holiday card and maybe a sports magnet, and calling it good? Oh yes, and don't forget those endless phone calls that we're supposed to make to check in and ask for referrals. Well, if you're like me—and we're being real here—you struggle with reaching out to your past clients and asking for referrals for a multitude of reasons (and excuses). When you don't take the time to make those phone calls, you find yourself scrambling to create the perfect storm where you can casually run into your past clients and innocently ask for referrals without sounding desperate, like a typical salesperson.

Maybe you're not like me, have no issue with reaching out, and don't need this structured system. Or maybe you'd just like a structured system to take the guesswork out of getting these referrals and getting a fifteen-to-one rate of return on your investment (ROI).

Remember, in the real estate world, a three- or four-to-one ROI is what we aim for. A five-to-one ROI is awesome, which is why a *fifteen-to-one ROI* is unheard of and also why I am sharing this program with you.

However you fit into the equation, this could possibly be what you've been waiting for to take your business to the next level. Let me start out by saying that this is an all-or-nothing endeavor that could be **the** game changer you've been looking for. Once launched, you can't half step it, or it will fail, miserably. I highly encourage you to read through this entire book before deciding whether or not this is for you. Launching the program and not following through will be more detrimental to your business than not starting at all. This is owing to the fact that you will be overpromising and under delivering. We all know this is people's number-one complaint about any business. For example, at the Ritz Carlton Club level, you are promised complimentary drinks and an amazing spread of appetizers every day at 4:00 p.m. Imagine heading to attend this special event for clients like you and discovering there was nothing set up for you. This is not an image you want to portray when people are entrusting you with their families', friends', neighbors', and even their own real estate needs.

Not only do people like feeling special, but people like relationships. They don't care for being on a drip campaign or a list that gets robocalled once or twice a year. The most important part of this program is *how you are making your past and present clients feel.* In the late Maya Angelou's wise words, *"I've learned that people will forget what you said, people will forget what you did, but people will never forget how you made them feel."* What better truth is there? The secret to transforming your business is to build a special relationship with a select group of your clients.

This system is a full-contact, all-or-nothing sport with a fifteen-to-one rate of return. This program is regimented but has the flexibility for every agent to make it his or her own. You will be belly to belly with your past, present, and future clients—a lot. It's very relationship- and connection-based, so if that's not your thing, then maybe cold-calling or prospecting is a better fit for you. I just know I'd rather have coffee with a past client and get a great referral that turns into a warm appointment than sit on the phone for two hours to land a cold appointment where I'm competing for business.

Ready to jump in?

One

Why This Model Works

Take out your wallet or key ring right now and count how many perks programs you have cards for. This isn't even counting the programs that don't give you cards to carry, like Marriott rewards or your airline high-miler club. All the big companies have clubs. Once you've earned the number of points needed to get into that exclusive club, you do your best to maintain your membership status and all its perks, right? You might be *heartbroken* knowing your rewards were about to run out, so you'd book a flight or purchase something to maintain your perk status, wouldn't you? This system—the one I'm about to outline in this book—isn't any different than any of those. You will create a "cool kids' club" for those special members in your database. The community created within that group will make them never want to leave. In essence, you will create your own tribe. The best part is, with the proper launch, commitment, and execution of the program, you will never have to outwardly (and, for most people, awkwardly) ask for a referral again. You may start to hear things like *"Oh my gosh, I really have to get you a referral ASAP!"* You may get text messages with random names and numbers or a shared contact followed up with a *"This is my sister-in-law. Call her. She wants to list her house and buy another."* The system shown here is set up so that your clients feel indebted to you and will naturally direct all of their referrals to you.

The basic rules of clubs still apply, and what makes your business different from everyone else's is—you guessed it—you have a *club* for *your* clients. Each and every one of your clients is welcome to join, and you'll discover that they'll work hard for you in order to keep their membership because they like the benefits. They like feeling special. And they are. They can become your business's most valuable assets.

Now, statistically speaking, your recent clients are probably not going to buy another house in the next three to five years, but that isn't why they are valuable to you. They have friends, families, work associates, church groups, children's sports teams, and more. They are, in short, happy clients who are a part of your club and are actively looking for people they can refer to you—other people who are looking to buy or sell a home. This is when your tribe members do a magical thing. To the person they know who is looking to buy or sell a home, they say, *"Oh, I know just the person to help you!"* Though you may only help a client buy a handful of homes over his or her lifetime, there is no limit to the number of referrals a client can send your way.

Owing to the structure of this specific system, you will be feeding into your clients' deep psychological need for connection—to feel as though they are valuable members of a community and a part of an exclusive membership club, a club that stems from contributions and rewards and includes such things as monthly giveaways. Your club members will not want to jeopardize their status or fall out of your good graces; therefore, they will remain loyal and constantly keep their eyes and ears open looking for referrals to send your way.

Now that you have a taste of what this system can do for you, it is time to think about what you need to have in place before you create your club. I highly recommend implementing this system when you have, or are about to have, an administrative assistant in place to run the back end of it. This program might seem like an endless parade of coffee dates, lunches, and happy hours, but much of this program requires scheduling, organization, and data entry. Those things seem to be the kryptonite of the rainmaker types. Even if you are a superman or superwoman, consider the fact that your business will be taking off with this approach, and you will need to keep up with the demand of new buyers and sellers in your pipeline, as well as fulfilling the promises of the program. You want to make the most efficient and effective use of your time. Having an admin helps significantly. Your admin can also be a sounding board for your ideas because two heads are usually better than one.

Think of this program as a garden. You need to hoe the rows, plant the seeds, water and tend to the plants, and wait for them to grow and provide fruits and vegetables. Sure, you could go to the market and buy all your produce, but what happens when someone else shows up before you and buys all the strawberries? Or what happens when a snap frost devastates the lettuce harvest? You never know what is going to be available when you go to the market. But when you've grown your own garden, it provides for you. Again and again. And if you tend it well, it overprovides.

Since the whole premise of this system is based on giving versus receiving, you are creating a culture of gratitude around your system, and we all know that great things come from gratitude. Here is where we input that saying, *"You get what you give."* Nothing rings more true than when people feel the gratitude you are showing for their loyalty evidenced by their referrals. They are going to want to keep feeling that emotion and keep feeding you more referrals.

Two

Branding

Who are you? Who are your clients? What is your business? What makes you stand out from the rest in your field? If your clientele and your business aren't what you want them to be, then implementing this system is a great time to rebrand yourself. These questions are important because the answers are the life of your business. You must come up with a brand for the exclusive club that you are going to invite your past clients and biggest fans to be a part of.

Choose a name, a logo, and a theme that fit your clientele or your desired clientele. There are many philosophies of branding and marketing, so I would encourage you to study up on those before your launch. There are several amazing books on branding at your fingertips (or on Amazon!), and I recommend reading one or more of them for a better understanding of how branding and marketing work.

Branding is the iconic message that is delivered to a customer in a heartbeat. It's a logo; it's a feeling you get when you are presented with a brand; it's a jingle that your kids sing out loud in the car, over and over again, without being aware of what noises they are making.

It's part of the overall impact a product, company, or service has on the customers and clients who interact with it. Branding is vitally important to your business—and not just because a solid brand makes it easy to communicate who you are to your customers but also because it makes it easy for them to *remember* who you are and what you do. When it comes time to tell their friends and family about you, your branding should make this communication easier.

Branding isn't about being the best, the most exclusive, or the most widely recognized. Branding is about customer satisfaction. Customers will gravitate toward a brand that makes them feel better about themselves and the world around them, something that makes them feel good about being part of a special community, and lastly, something they can identify with. The long and the short of it all is that the brand of your club should match your current branding and should sound attractive to your clientele.

I want to show you how branding can look different by sharing the stories of three individual realtors who learned about this program and then applied their unique approaches to the system. These agents are Roberta, Larry, and Jennifer. These are "stereotypical" types of agents; we all know agents like them in our offices or in our marketplaces.

First, let's talk about Roberta. She is a very elegant woman who has been in the business for twenty-five years and has no plans to retire soon. Since she is primarily a "luxury" agent, many of her transactions occur in golf-course and country-club communities. Roberta describes her clients as "exclusive" and "VIP." Most of her business is done by referral, and she's also recently hired a business coach to help her leave the legacy she wants to her family.

The coach tells her that with the number of people in her database and all of the business models she has used, she should be getting a much higher rate of return. The coach suggests *this* unique program. After attending a seminar about the program, she decides a branding of Crown Jewels will fit well. That branding will allow for multiple levels of her program such as Diamond, Sapphire, and Emerald that would appeal to her high-end, luxury clientele and the lifestyle brand she has already created in her business.

Next is our friend, Larry. Larry is the big personality who has been in the business about ten years. This guy is a mover and a shaker, always wearing a suit and driving a luxury car. He is always shaking hands and kissing babies—the politician type. Larry is very direct and doesn't always give off a warm and fuzzy vibe. Larry struggles to understand why he doesn't get more referrals when he sells homes in such a short time, usually over list price. He believes people should choose him based on his performance alone. He stays in touch by utilizing automatic-drip campaigns and football schedules.

Business was great when the market was down because he went after expireds and short sales, but as the market improved and those expireds and short sales became more scarce, that well began to run dry, and he saw his competition closing much more than he was. Larry farms a community of starter homes in his local area, and his average price point is just below the average in his local marketplace. He does great work and helps many families year after year, but he'd like more repeat and referral business instead of the daily grind of prospecting or paying through the nose for new Internet leads.

Larry's new coach, like Roberta's, told him that for as many years in the business as he had (as well as his huge database), he should be getting more referrals. Attending the same seminar as Roberta, Larry decided his "Larry's Club" could consist of Premier, Elite, and VIP client levels. His clients are hardworking, blue-collar people who live modestly, such as teachers, union workers, and so on. He feels that branding makes his clients feel special.

Last and surely not least, let's take a look at Jennifer. She has been in the business about eight years, has always done well, and is very social, especially in her neighborhood, where she believes the party doesn't start til she walks in. Although she's received a lot of training in cold calling, it is her least favorite thing to do. She's much more comfortable going to a party, talking a little real estate, and hoping for referrals from her friends and acquaintances who know she's a REALTOR. She was trained early in her career to work by referral but never felt quite comfortable enough to ask for it, nor did she like "popping by" unannounced to clients' homes with random "gifts."

Owing to the work Jennifer did before her real estate career, much of her clientele includes down-to-earth, blue-collar folks with money. These are family-oriented people who like their sports; her sphere includes many cops, firefighters, and people in other blue-collar jobs.

Jennifer's coach points out that she is not getting the referrals she should be, considering the reach and depth of her database. Jennifer never had a systematic way of staying in touch with her clients other than a monthly drip campaign, the yearly sports schedule, and, on a good year, a Christmas card.

When Jennifer (who is really me) started her program, she liked the idea of VIPs but realized that "VIP" sounded a little stuffy to her blue-collar-with-money clientele. MVP was something that these hard-working, down-to-earth, sports-loving clients would relate to. So, her program branding included MVPs, All-Stars, and Winner's Circle. This marketing strategy fit Jennifer because it can be bold, like her, and it gets to the point.

Maybe your program has something that fits well with your current branding, such as Bill Round's Inner Circle. Or, if you specialize in condo sales or units in city skyscrapers, maybe your marketing will focus around the penthouse or concierge levels. The possibilities really are endless. The point is that you need to know your clients (and desired clients) and find something that they will find attractive but that also matches the image you have already been conveying to them. You will want to choose something that you can have multiple levels or tiers as you will sort in a later chapter.

Three

Who Gets to Be in Your Tribe?

Once you have a brand established, the next step is figuring out who is worthy of being in your tribe. At the time I created and began implementing this system, I had well over fifteen hundred people in my database. I had to set some parameters for who would get to be in my MVP (client appreciation) program. To me, MVP stands for *"my valuable partner."* These are people who have done business with me, have referred business to me, or whom I know for a fact would refer me or hire me if the opportunity arose. In some way, shape, or form, I feel confident that I am *their* Realtor, not anyone else. I am not **A** Realtor they refer to; I am **THE** Realtor they refer to.

For obvious reasons, I do not add people who are not fond of me. We've all had *those* clients, the ones who, once the transaction is over and closed, we cannot wait to delete from our phones and whom we are thankful we don't have to speak to again. Those people don't *get* to be in your tribe.

What about those friends, past clients, and associates who might have another *THE* Realtor? This might sound crazy, but you could always pick up the phone and ask them, right? Give them a call, tell them what you are putting together, and see if they are interested in being a part of *your* tribe. If you do, just advise them the only "requirement" is that they don't have another Realtor to whom they refer business, that you are the *only* Realtor they will be referring people to.

Now how about those clients with whom you haven't talked in a while? Take Bob and Susan. They bought a house with you seven years ago, but you haven't spoken since. So add them. If they want nothing to do with you, they will either not respond to your e-mails, or they will unsubscribe altogether. If they have fond memories of you and don't realize that seven years have flown by, they will be happy to hear from you, and they just might throw a referral your way—or even be ready to do business themselves. This has happened to me several times over.

Do people get dropped from the club? Absolutely, but this happens on a case-by-case basis, and sometimes they even self-select out of the program. My admin and I do an audit once every six months or so to see if anyone needs to be pulled from the group. Honestly, this has only happened a few times. Maybe I saw someone's house listed by someone else or saw on Facebook that a former client bought a house and not from me. Is that the determining factor, and they are automatically kicked out? No! I have someone in my MVP program who refers her friends to me but is obliged to use her family-friend Realtor for herself. That's okay with me because I understand the predicament she is in. As the program grew over the years, we needed to slim down our tribe in order to continue to manage my time and efforts successfully. We sent out an e-mail that said since we had grown, those who hadn't given a referral in five years would no longer qualify for our MVP program; however, they could come back at any time just by giving us a referral.

Momentum is an important part of this program. Once people get a taste of what it is like to progress in the program, they're going to come back for more. It's a natural inclination, and, in fact, there is even a term for it: *gamification*. Gamification is the practice of using aspects of game design and strategies in nongame environments and, in doing so, helping to improve user interaction and retention, increase productivity and organization, and drive recruitment. This sort of experience is tied into what is called a feedback loop—you do something, you get a reward, and so you do it again. Your tribe will talk about your program to others, who will want to get in on the fun. Word spreads. More clients show up, hoping for a chance to participate. They have a good experience and go back to the person who told them, which reinforces the first party's effort to engage these folks, and so on and so forth.

Although we have a closed Facebook group for our MVPs, I do post tidbits about our MVP program on my regular Facebook page from time to time, like photos from our Date Night event that showed everyone having a great time, or a picture of the Paint and Sip party with all of the works of art we created. Non-MVPs will comment things like, "How did I not hear about this?!" Then I get the opportunity to tell them that it was for my elite tribe of MVPs and explain what constitutes an MVP. The attendees also will tag me in their posts, thanking me for this or that with a photo of what they are thanking me for. The MVPs feel a part of this elite community, and I can post things they will want to know about. All of these things create a buzz around the program and make people long for a chance to get in on the action.

Four

Gifts: Purpose and Ideas

The point of this whole model, after all, is to generate opportunities to spend some actual physical time with your clients. All of your program partners are invited to participate in the monthly giveaway or event while the ongoing reward is reserved for the highest tier group. We will elaborate more on the different tiers in a moment.

First of all, it's not about the gift. Well, maybe it's a little bit about the gift. Allow me to explain. The true purpose of the gift is to have a reason to reach out to your clients every month and then see different clients throughout the year. On the same day every month (I chose the first of the month because it was easiest for me), you'll be sending out an e-mail to everyone in your group about the monthly giveaway. Depending on the size of your group and the size of your budget, you'll have anywhere from five to twenty-five gifts to dole out

The other purpose of this monthly giveaway is to have an excuse to e-mail your people about something fun every month. Yes, they'll get their regular real estate "market update" e-mail every month, but the people you've included in this special program will get another e-mail every month. Why e-mail and not just a Facebook notification? It's simple: I want this special group of clients to get in the habit of opening my e-mails. If all I send are real estate–related e-mails, and they aren't planning on buying or selling a home anytime soon, they might unsubscribe from my e-mails or mark them as junk; then I've lost touch with the very people I want to connect to. I want them to associate seeing my name in their e-mail inbox with happiness, gratitude, and good stuff!

THE MONTHLY GIVEAWAY

Yes, we said it is not about the gift but rather getting face-to-face time with your clients. This being said, the gift *does* have to be something valuable enough that your clients will cheerfully spend their time to come get it from you. When deciding on a gift, always ask yourself, "Would I sacrifice time from *my* lunch hour to go pick it up from someone else's office?" When I set up my MVP program, I identified 170 people who would be included, and I thought that I should have fifteen items for the taking.

Well, lesson learned. Fifteen was too many. The second month, I lowered the number of items to ten. Now that I have about 220 people in my MVP program, I do twelve to fifteen gifts a month. How many gifts should you have every month? That depends on your market and your clientele, but remember that each interaction with a client can take an hour or more. While this time is valuable and well spent, you can't spend all of your time having face-to-face time with these clients. Keep in mind these are people who aren't actively looking to buy or sell a house. These partners are helping you *find* clients who are actually buying or selling. You don't need to have face-to-face time with these clients more than once or twice a year. You are e-mailing them once a month (or more) already.

You're never too far from their minds as it is. You don't have to be that person who shows up every month with a freshly baked pie, begging to be allowed to hang out for dinner.

You have to think about whether the gifts match *your* brand. Will your group love them? Are they helpful and enriching their lives or really just junk? Are they good enough that people will go out of their way to come get them from you at your office or meet you for lunch to get them? Think about what kinds of things your clients would see or use regularly. These items don't have to have your name on them, but when your clients see gifts from you, they should think of you, consciously or subconsciously, and then you will be on their minds when the topic of real estate is brought up.

While Roberta's folks would probably appreciate a free round of golf at the country club or a fantastic bottle of champagne out of a case she stumbled across, perhaps Larry's people would prefer tickets to a sporting event or some beer growlers with a free-fill certificate. I'm betting Jennifer's tribe could go either way.

Think of this as the "pop in" rather than the "pop by." You aren't having to wander all over town dropping off inexpensive goodies that your clients may not even want or items that may not fit their personalities or lifestyles. You don't have to show up unannounced at their homes to discover that they aren't there or are too busy to chat. Your clients are setting up a specific time to meet with you—on your turf—to pick up their monthly gifts. I prefer my clients to come to my office because it is a big, beautiful commercial space that lets them know I am a professional.

Of course, like everything, there are exceptions. I might have a client who is elderly or recently injured. In this case, I would plan a time to stop by his home. Or maybe I just spent some time with a client at her baby shower a couple of weeks ago, and we don't need to spend an hour to connect, so I can drop off her gift on my way home from work. Just be sure that in general, people do not expect you to leave these gifts on their doorsteps like a package delivery service. That would defeat the whole purpose: that you're creating opportunities for face-to-face time with your clients.

When thinking about what gifts to offer, try to think about things with a good shelf life that you can keep handy in your garage. Things happen, and sometimes that gift you really wanted to give away that month falls through. You absolutely cannot skip a month, or it ruins your credibility, so ALWAYS have a backup plan and a backup gift ready to go.

Something else to keep in mind is that you can also create co-branded opportunities with local businesses. This is where you'd strike a deal with a local business owner to score gift certificates that are cobranded where you will only get charged for the gift certificate if it is used. I have a travel agent who creates amazing, stress-free Disney vacations and charges a fifty-dollar consult fee. I gave out forty cobranded gift certificates that had an expiration date six months out, and she agreed to only charge me the fifty dollars when someone redeemed one. My travel agent was appreciative of my efforts to grow her business. I gave some of my clients a fifty-dollar item of value, and in the end, I spent nothing because no one redeemed one. It was a win-win-win.

THE SPECIAL EVENTS
A few times a year, you should host an event instead of offering a gift. That month, their admission to the event becomes the gift. You will end up spending a little more money on these events, but you will also get great quality time with your clients and build community at the same time. Some of the events we have done in the past are painting parties, date nights, mini photo sessions, and sporting events. Again, always remember who your clients are and

what they'll appreciate. Are you like Larry and his clientele, where maybe a fun bowling party would be something that people would want to attend? Or maybe you're more like Roberta, for whom a champagne and caviar-tasting event would be more appropriate? The way it sounds, Jennifer would probably have a huge hit with a wine-tasting or beer-tasting event.

To get the best bang for your buck on these events, pay attention to sites like LivingSocial, Groupon, and Goldstar. We used a Groupon for a paint-night event at a local pub for about twenty people, and we opened a tab at the bar for people to order their first drink on me. That night turned out to be a blast. Each person could be in his or her own element, and it allowed me to have one-on-one time with each person there, really connecting.

Our date-night event was also fun. We talked our local taproom into allowing our crowd of twenty-five to thirty people to take over their space. We bought each of the attendees two drinks, and we gave each couple two free movie tickets and a pamphlet showcasing the schedule of movies at the theater right across the street. To our extra-special attendees, those who were currently in the All-Star or Winner's Circle tier, we also gave a large bag of Lindor truffles. In addition, we had a wheel that we got from the dollar store that we used to give out a couple of extra prizes. The night was a great success and gave us quality time with our clients. On top of that, none of the attendees left to go to the movies; they had so much fun, they actually shut the place down, and I was the first one to leave.

Mini photo sessions can also be a great way to generate interest in your exclusive club. Almost everyone wants a photo shoot with family or loved ones, especially around the holidays. Timing is crucial on this one, especially when thinking about what your theme will be. For example, we did our last photo shoot at the end of

October, when there were still a few fall colors left and the air was nice and crisp for photo attire. This left people ample time to use these photos for their holiday cards if they desired to do so.

With this type of event, look for your talented friends or a local photographer who has her system down because this one is not quite as easy as it sounds. You have to run an organized, tight ship to keep everyone happy. We scheduled three time blocks, and it was first-come, first-served within each time block. Those who were awaiting their turns were treated to a beverage of their choice from the adjoining coffee shop. This gave us time to discuss what was happening in their lives and what possible referrals they might have for me.

Another big hit has been our Mariners' baseball night for our most elite tier called our Winner's Circle. Along with one of our favorite lenders, we were able to treat a group of forty people to a pro baseball game on a special giveaway night. Owing to cost, we chose to do the terrace level instead of renting out a suite. The private suites were approximately $10,000, but grabbing a whole section in the terrace level ended up being $2,000, half of which was paid by our lender, who also attended and scored face time with the clients. Those seats were $50 each because we bought forty, but they retail for $100 a piece because the level of service is a bit higher than in regular box seats. The opportunity this gave us to connect with folks was fantastic. Everyone was happy, and we watched the referrals flood in. Like we said earlier, once people get a taste of the "good life," they will do anything they can to stay in your club.

Since these events tend to be big-budget ordeals, you need to constantly remind your attendees of the commitment. Schedule reminder e-mails, make phone calls early in the week leading up to your event, and remind, remind, remind! People around you at these events will start to notice what you're doing and ask for your business card, especially at events that are held in public places, like that Mariners' game we just mentioned. We picked up a client who was simply curious about the group we had for the game. It was a perfect opportunity to tell him about my business and, of course, my program.

You want to be purposeful. You want face time. You also want to make sure your crowd (especially your top referral sources) is engaged. Find something that pushes your clients' hot button. Do they drink? What are their passions? Use that knowledge to find that sweet spot in the referral machine. When your clients feel appreciated and recognized, the sky's the limit for referrals. Your events can range from a cocktail party to a volunteer day—whatever your specific crowd desires. If you have a diverse crowd, try to keep your event local to your market. The opportunity to go local and support local can mean a bigger return for engagement. *How you contribute to your community speaks volumes.* Remember, you get what you give. Sometimes it's not just about the gift but the dedication and consistency in all that you do.

Five

Budget

Oh the big, bad B word. But your budget is an important factor to take into consideration as you plan your program. We might as well get this out of the way up front: you're going to be spending money on this program, even if you manage to get all of your monthly gifts for free (which you won't). There is good news, though. You will be setting up a budget for this program at a level that you feel comfortable with—and it should form part of your marketing budget.

As with all things, scale your expectations and investment. Let's say you're giving away ten to twenty gifts every month. If you spend $10 on each gift, you're looking at a budget of $100 to $200 per month ($1200 or $2400 a year). When you are shopping for items, plan on negotiating a deal. One of the best ways to secure unique and fabulous gifts is to plan ahead and work with other local businesses. Remember, you're going to be introducing your clients to these local businesses. That's an important piece of your negotiation with the business. These gifts aren't just about you; they're also about the local businesses and how you support your community. You will be introducing your clients to a business that they may have never heard of, and after sampling what that new business has to offer, they could become new clients for that business. The bottom line is that you want to give away something of value—without paying full price. Buy out of season; buy in bulk; buy gift certificates at a discounted rate, knowing that customers tend to spend more than the amount of the gift certificate when they actually redeem it.

Gifts can be gateway opportunities. You don't have to spend money on a whole experience for your clients. Spend enough to get them to try something they might not have otherwise have chosen. Give them reasons to be adventurous. Everyone has a cupboard full of coffee cups, but how many of them have actually gone to a pottery shop and made their own? For instance, I once negotiated with a local golf course for 50 percent off the cost of a round of golf because I pointed out that the clients who got this discount card would probably bring some friends (who golfs alone, right?) and they'd probably rent a cart, as well as spending some time at the clubhouse and in the pro shop. Whatever amount the golf course lost on the price of the round of golf, they would certainly make up for in other purchases made that day by these customers.

We have had great success negotiating deals on our monthly giveaways. You might be able to get a case of books at ten dollars each, even when those books retail for twenty-five dollars each. For Valentine's Day, we were able to get twelve dozen roses for $144 (twelve dollars per bouquet) that would normally cost upward of twenty to thirty dollars a dozen.

I have also had great luck with the home-based, direct sales businesses run by my friends and even past clients. One friend sells jewelry, and I was able to purchase several pairs of earrings that we gave away in May for a Mother's Day–inspired gift. They retailed for thirty-eight dollars a pair, and I was able to secure them for nine dollars a pair when they went on clearance. You might have to shine up your negotiating skills and show vendors how this really is a win for everyone, but these are great opportunities.

There are deals everywhere. You just have to work a little harder to find them, and if you have a budget that you're trying to work within, it will force you to be a little clever in your spending. This cleverness will translate to more interesting gifts that will catch your clients' attention. However, this isn't all the money you're going to spend on this program. There's also the matter of funding the rewards portion of the program, which will be covered in the next chapter.

Six

All Stars, Rewards and RESPA Too

You've now decided whom you are going to invite to be a part of your program, and you've figured out a plan for your monthly giveaways. You have a means by which you are going to regularly interact with these select partners—via monthly giveaway e-mails and reminder phone calls about upcoming events. So what's next?

Before we talk about the magic, let's talk about the elephant in the room in regards to gifts and such. I'm talking about Section 8 of RESPA (the Real Estate Settlement Procedures Act), which states that no real estate agent shall offer gifts or rewards with the intention of influencing, closing, or funding any real estate transaction. To be clear, *all gifts and rewards of this program are related to the referral of clients to my office for potential business.* It's not the job of my clients to close a transaction. That's my job. They are partnering to help me find potential clients. It's important to remember this distinction when you're implementing your program so that you don't run afoul of the rules of doing good business. We have done our due diligence to be sure we are RESPA compliant.

So then, how *does* the magic work? It's all about referrals. Even now, when your former clients refer you new clients, they get rewarded. It's as simple as that. However, it is not really that simple, is it? Did you remember to send Tom a gift for referring his cousin Joe? Did you already reward Stacy for choosing you over the other agent? Wait, you remember buying that thank-you card and the flowers, but who were they for again? Did you ever put that card in the mail? Luckily, we have a system for rewards that will be practically foolproof! Is this method a little complicated? Yes, it is, and that is why we mentioned earlier the importance of having an admin in place to keep this in check.

We decided to call the second tier in our program the All-Star level. Since we are an office full of women, it isn't very common for us to go all-out on a sports theme, but that is who our clientele are, and we ALWAYS put our clients' needs and wants first!

The All-Star level of the program is for people who give you a referral or who are self-referred. As soon as you receive a referral from anyone, mark it down somewhere to keep an eye on it. My team uses Google Drive and Google Sheets so we can all access our documents from wherever we are in the world, as long as we have Wi-Fi access. The rule we decided to implement is that the person who is referred to me has to meet with me in person before I make the referring party an All-Star. Again, there are obviously some exceptions for referrals that might be coming from a distance, but for those, as long as there has been some sort of buyer consultation or listing presentation, the referrer is welcomed to the next level of the club.

WHAT ARE THE ALL-STAR REWARDS?

Once it is official, your new second tier will get a Starbucks card branded to your program. We chose a ten-dollar card. Since our budget was tighter when we started the program, we chose to have a company create stickers that were the exact size and shape of the Starbucks card so we could overlay them onto the cards. Starbucks also has a program where you can have them brand a card for you, but I believe there is an approximately $2000 setup fee.

Does it have to be Starbucks? Of course not! Starbucks cards work for my program for a few reasons. First, the cards themselves are free. Second, as I am a Starbucks gold-card holder, I end up getting perks like free treats, coffee, additional coupons, and offers just because I funnel my business through that card. So not only are my All-Stars getting perks, so am I. A third reason Starbucks works for us is all about location. We are based about thirty minutes south of Seattle, Washington, the Starbucks capital of the world. The Northwest is known for having one of the greatest percentages of coffee drinkers in the general population, and for those who aren't big coffee drinkers, there are many other products my clients can buy from Starbucks. However, if Starbucks doesn't fit your clientele, I'm sure you will be creative enough to find a system or reward that fits *your* brand.

When we present our All-Star members with their cards, usually via USPS or hand-delivered, they are also given an insert that explains the program. They also receive a follow-up e-mail with the same information. They are informed that the card will be automatically loaded with ten dollars a month for six months. The most important note that you need to share with them is that they cannot transfer the funds from their cards to their mobile app or to any other Starbucks account that they might have. Explain that this makes reloading (almost) impossible. I say "almost" because my admin is pretty good at what she does and would find a way to do it no matter what, but it's not in our best interests to have clients moving funds from our branded cards anyway.

Even if these clients only ever give me the one referral that got them into the All-Star tier, they can benefit from upward of seventy dollars of free Starbucks. Some people still just don't use the money, and when their six months expire, we transfer the remaining funds back to my main gold card and remove the client's card from the account card catalogue. They also receive an e-mail letting them know that their card has expired, but not to worry because they are still a part of the MVP program, and they will receive the perks of that program. For those super fabulous All-Stars of mine who see that their time having these perks is nearly up and send another referral my way, they are automatically given a twenty-five-dollar bonus, and their cardholder status is extended another six months from the time I meet with their referral.

Most of the instructions and explanations that the new card-holders receive are in the e-mail we send out when we send their cards to them. We have also sent these cards in handwritten note-cards that have a slip of paper with the CliffsNotes' version of the instructions. I have included a template of that slip at the end of this book.

Again, it is important to stress to your clients that they can't transfer their card funds unless they want this to be a one-time deal—just one ten-dollar reward. You want them not to transfer funds from the cards you've given them because at the end of their term (whether that's just six months or longer), you will want to be able to transfer the remaining balance back to your main gold card, as well as all recuperate the points that they have earned by spending the money on the card, which is under your account. This means YOU get the perks. Since I started this program, I literally haven't paid for drinks or food at Starbucks in a couple of years. I always have a free reward or two waiting for me on my account. So yes, the initial expense might seem a little daunting, but this number will dwindle, not only because of the free perks you will receive but also as a result of those people who don't use their cards much (or at all) and thus leave you a balance to transfer back to your account at the end of the term. These will be dollars that you will be able to use for the next month's reloads.

So do you have to use Starbucks? Absolutely not, but as I mentioned earlier, we are in the Pacific Northwest, and we LOVE our coffee up here, so it was an easy decision for us. I'm sure there are plenty more companies that this program could work with, but I have honestly never looked into it because Starbucks fits my clientele so perfectly. Even if clients don't drink coffee, I just remind them that Starbucks also serves tea and food—and some are even serving wine now. I even have a couple of clients who save up all of their funds until they get the e-mail reminding them that their card is near its expiration, and then they go in and buy a large retail item, like a French press.

WHEN AND HOW EXACTLY DOES SOMEONE BECOME AN ALL-STAR?

Here are a couple of scenarios that keep you within the guidelines of RESPA.

SCENARIO 1

Bob calls me and tells me he gave my card to his friend Carl at work. I say thank you so much and remind him that once I connect with Carl in an appointment, then Bob will be a part of my MVP program. If he's already an MVP, I explain that this referral will bump him up to the All-Star level. The point of this is that Bob will put pressure on Carl to call me because he wants to be an All-Star.

Carl calls me, and we chat about him buying a home. I tell Carl he needs to get preapproved for a mortgage first, and once he does that, we'll meet for a buyer consultation. Bob is still not yet an All-Star because this initial chat is not enough. Then Carl gets preapproved, and we meet for a consult. Bob is now an All-Star, whether or not Carl ever buys a house from me.

My ability to close Carl is not Bob's responsibility. That's my job. Bob did his job by getting me a legitimate referral. Is Carl an All-Star? Not yet. Carl will become an All-Star once we get a contract on a home written up.

SCENARIO 2

Gail refers me to her sister, Karen, who wants to sell her house and is interviewing a few agents for the job. I thank Gail, just as I did Bob in the above scenario, and I give her the same explanation about how she'll join my MVP program or move up a level once I meet with Karen. Karen and I have a meeting since I am now (thanks to Gail) one of three agents she is interviewing. Gail, if she's already an MVP, becomes an All-Star that day whether or not Karen chooses me. Karen becomes an All-Star as well, once she has signed a listing agreement with me.

Yes, I've read Section 8 of RESPA quite a few times and had two different managing brokers look over my program. Both of them gave it their "complying with RESPA" blessings. I highly suggest you read Section 8 of RESPA for yourself for when some of your colleagues or competitors try to call you out for violating RESPA by using this program. You can politely tell them that you are not tying gifts or rewards to any funding or closings; therefore, you are in compliance.

HOW DOES THE STARBUCKS CARD SYSTEM WORK FOR THE ALL-STAR TIER?

On your online Starbucks gold-card account, you will "add a card" to your account. This is free. You will add the recipient's name, card number, and security code before giving the card to the recipient.

You do this beforehand so you can make sure you've got the correct numbers in the system. There's nothing more embarrassing than having to ask a client, "Hey, can I get you to read the number of that card for me, so I can reload your card?" You will need a system that keeps track of those contacts who have achieved All-Star status. We have found that Google Sheets (like Excel) works for us. Often times the biggest cheerleaders need extensive notes and dates on the spreadsheet to show their multiple referrals. Keep track! This program only works well if your, or your admin's, tracking skills are completely on point.

Our cards are reloaded every month on the first of the month (for six months). It is imperative that you do it on the same day each month because humans like consistency, and it reminds them that you always fulfill your promises. From your online Starbucks gold-card account, you will transfer the amount of funds you choose to each recipient individually. Our system is ten dollars per month so, depending on the number of recipients, you'll need to make sure your gold card has the appropriate balance for transferring to everyone. Note that the Starbucks website only allows you to load a hundred dollars to your gold card per day. You can physically go into the Starbucks store and load your card with a barista, at which point you could load the amount you'll need for the entire list—although even in person, there is a maximum balance of $500. Always keep a buffer of fifty dollars or more on your account as you never know when you'll need to automatically load the promised twenty-five dollar bonus.

For expired All-Stars, the rule is that you will transfer their unused funds from their cards back to your main gold card. This is why it is important to stress that they should not move the card funds on their program-connected Starbucks card to their personal accounts, as you will not be able to reclaim the funds if they do. After each card is loaded or expired, you will send an e-mail reminding clients that their cards have been reloaded or expired. When you are sending this e-mail, you are also reminding them, on a subconscious level, that you are their awesome Realtor who would love their referrals.

Here are a few notes for your admin. Keep a Google Sheets or Excel spreadsheet of all of the expired Starbucks cards on a separate tab or sheet so you can refer back to them. This is a crucial step because sometimes one of your MVPs (who was once an All-Star) refers you another lead; it just happens that more than six months have passed since the last lead they gave you, so that card is currently inactive. It is very easy to reactivate the card this MVP had (if he or she didn't throw it away) if you still have the card number and the verification code from the back. This will save you a bit of money by not having to acquire more cards to give out, and it encourages your clients to keep their program-connected Starbucks card around even if there is no money on it. In addition, it's a card with *your* branding that they have to carry around, which their friends may potentially see. I have my own Starbucks card and account, but I put one of my MVP stickers on it so I get more opportunities to talk about my program and my services as a real estate agent.

Seven

The Launch Phase

If you're still with me and ready to embark on this system, now is time to think about your carefully crafted launch. You can't just start this by randomly sending out e-mails to a nonspecific selection of people in your sphere of influence to offer an arbitrary gift and expect it to work. You will likely confuse people and not get the kind of response you need or want.

Your first step is to decide who gets to be a member of the club. We discussed earlier (in chapter 3) who gets to be an MVP, but the general rule is that members should be those people whom you feel confident would call you if they, or someone they know, needed real estate services. I composed my initial group from the following types:

1. All past clients but only the ones I'd want to do business with again.
2. Anyone who had ever tried to refer me, whether it worked out or not.
3. People I KNEW would refer me if given the opportunity to, and I know they do not already have a Realtor they refer business to. These people might have said something like, "Oh, I'm so glad we met. Now I have a realtor to refer to!"

My original list was somewhere around 175 people—but keep in mind, this can still work if your list is only ten people. Expect it to grow fairly quickly.

After you have figured out your list of MVPs, you need to let them know about this new and exciting addition to your business. It is important to emphasize that this program is about *them* and not *you*.

Your messages about your program should impart the feeling that you are grateful for their business, their referrals, and their re-peat business, and that you are now going to make it *your* business to show that gratitude by offering them items of value each month.

Be sure that your message doesn't convey the idea that *"I'm go-ing to spend money on you because I believe it will get you to give me referrals."* This is the opposite of what you want. You need to really embrace this philosophy or else your less-than-genuine inten-tions will seep into your messages. People will sense that you don't really care about them; you just care about cashing the checks that come from their referrals.

With the launch, you should be looking to generate approxi-mately eight touches in eight weeks (an eight-by-eight approach). After eight weeks, you can drop back to the monthly or semimonthly mailings, but in the initial weeks, you want to be sure you frequently remind your members of the program and how it works.

People are busy, and sometimes they don't like extra e-mail, or they've got filters on their inboxes, which means it will likely take a few tries before you can be confident that they have received your messages. When you run into your clients, you don't want them to stare at you blankly when you talk about their participation in the program. In fact, let's hope they talk to you and tell you how excited they are to be partners.

The underlying message in these first touches should be your ongoing gratitude for their business, their referrals, and their repeat business. *Your program is the mechanism by which you show that gratitude, over and over again.* The message is NOT "Hey, I just bought some trinkets for you, so now you'll give me referrals, right?" A natural return on your investment will be clients coming to you with new business and referrals.

The first touch should be an official announcement letter, which should be sent on official letterhead. In these days of hyperconnectivity and electronic communication, a physical letter has become a rarity and is something that people still respond well to.

Naturally, the second touch should be an electronic version of this same announcement, sent a few days after the print letter has been received. If your new program members are going to respond to your letter (and a response isn't necessary, of course), they're more likely to do so via electronic means. While the printed letter is a more personal touch, responding in the same fashion is more complicated and time-consuming than dashing off an e-mail saying, "Got it. This looks like fun!"

Your third touch should be a personal one, typically by phone. This gives you an opportunity to talk directly about the program and about their involvement in the program. Do they have questions? Are they excited about the opportunity to be partners? Do they have ideas about gifts or events or other aspects of the program that could be helpful to you? Remember, they're also looking for opportunities to enrich their communities. Give them that opportunity.

The fourth touch should include the creation of some community around your program. Let your clients know they are part of a select group, and let them interact with other members of that group. Create a group in a readily available electronic community like Facebook, but don't forget to make it a closed group—it is key that the group be invitation only! Give yourself a few weeks to accomplish all of this as this will allow your clients time to see these touches, consider them, and respond to them.

The second wave of touches should be focused on talking about the benefits of membership in the program. The fifth touch should be an announcement to the group about the first monthly giveaway. The sixth and seventh touches should be through other means of communication that you use for your business—your business blog, your business Facebook page, your personal Facebook page. These touches are letting the rest of the world know about your group. Talk about how someone gets into the group, and describe the benefits of being in the group. These touches will remind those who are in the program already that they're part of something cool and exclusive, without talking to them directly about the program. (You've already done that a few times, right?) These touches are all about building buzz about your program. You want to get people talking about your program, and not just the MVPs. You want other folks asking these people what the fuss is about.

Finally, the eighth touch should be a reminder of the program's overall focus and goals, which can be tied in with the announcement of the second monthly giveaway.

At this point, you've been in your MVPs inbox once a week for about two months. They're now primed to look for regular communications from you in regards to this program. All you have to do is keep prompting them to participate in your giveaways and maintaining their exclusive status within the program.

Remember to make this sound fun and exciting and point out there is no other obligation than to meet up with you to pick up their gifts or at events that they have RSVPed for.

As your program grows, you will start to notice that the cream rises to the top. You may want to start rewarding your top 20 percent more than your other program participants. The people in this group are people who have done business with you multiple times, referred multiple family members and friends, and are your biggest cheerleaders out in the marketplace. These are people who deserve your best perks, and this is the level that needs to be scrutinized the most. To initially narrow down who should participate in this group, take the full number of contacts in your sphere or database and the number of people in your tier 1, MVP group. Calculate 20 percent of that group. That number is the maximum number of participants in your third tier. Obviously, there are exceptions for everything, but these people are your referral machines. They are your proof of the Pareto principle: 80 percent of business comes from 20 percent of your people. This top tier will get special treatment, and you want to keep these people in your corner. You will want to come up with a fun name for this exclusive group. In my case, I deemed my elite—my third tier—the "Winner's Circle" since that fit my sports' theme.

The Mariners' game I mentioned earlier was an event only for our Winner's Circle members. This was an event that was shared on Facebook and drew a TON of attention to the elite referral sources in our program. So many of our MVPs saw an event that they hadn't been invited to, and they wanted in! Sometimes that is the best way to get interest.

Another way to draw attention to these top tier members can be explained using a story about one of our MVP monthly give-aways—and remember that members of the Winner's Circle are of course still MVPs.

One February, we scored a great deal on rose bouquets. We advertised them as our MVP giveaway. In the same e-mail, we noted that for our Winner's Circle members, we would hand-deliver them on the fourteenth to the recipient of their choice (within a reasonable distance.) This drew quite a bit of attention, and it became a fabulous opportunity to talk about how our MVPs could rise to the top and get those perks also.

Eight

E-Mail Communication and Checklists

You will want to use an e-mail system other than your standard Outlook. Whether it is Mailchimp, Bombbomb, or Infusionsoft (or whatever works for you), just make sure to have an e-mail system in place that allows you to create lists, easily add images, tracks when the e-mails are opened, and is efficient. You will want to have a steady system for sending your e-mails to mass recipients. Keep your e-mails consistent in design. Touching back on branding, you want to keep things consistent so that your crowd will keep you in the back of their minds at all times. E-mails should be sent on the same day and at the same time every month. My e-mail system lets me schedule and group my messages so that the e-mail hits when people expect it.

In the e-mail system you choose, you'll want to create lists for each tier so you can easily choose the list of people you want to send the corresponding e-mail template to. The All-Star list, your second tier, will have to be closely monitored and edited at least once a month. New members will come in and be dropped out every month. The Winner's Circle should be updated at least once a quarter to see whom your referral machines are and aren't. The MVPs we try to do semiannually. In the client-relationship management

(CRM) we use, we're able to tag our MVPs and All-Stars. This is helpful for when you need to clean house, which you'll want to do about every six months, if not more frequently. A CRM, or list, is crucial and will need to be closely maintained across the programs you use. For example, if you use Top Producer (a type of CRM tool), the lists of MVPs and All-Stars you have on Top Producer should match the lists you have in your mail system (Bombbomb, Mailchimp, Infusionsoft, and so on). When a list is reorganized in one system, it should be reorganized in the other as well. You'll also need to create a reminder system/checklist in your business for when you get new referrals or meet new clients. Do they get added to the MVP e-mail list? Are they also All-Stars? Oh, not yet—so set a reminder to check if they do become All-Stars.

THIS IS IMPORTANT!

You can't announce that if someone gets you a referral, they'll become an All-Star with All-Star perks and then forget to follow through. This goes back to what I said in the introduction about the fact that this is an *all-or-nothing program*. This is also why you might want to have an admin on board for these tasks, as they are very time-consuming and time-sensitive.

Nine

Conclusion

This program will transform the way you interact with both your clients and your community, which is an important part of your place within the local economy. You are a bridge between individuals and their larger community. By embracing that connectivity through this program, you will be rewarded, time and again, by both your clients and your local businesses. Participate in your community. Give your clients face-to-face time. When your clients feel appreciated, the sky's the limit as far as what they will do for you. How you contribute to your community speaks more about you than nearly anything else you can do. Remember, you get what you give, and as long as you apply yourself with dedication and consistency, you will find your investments returned many times over.

Good luck!

Appendix A: Introduction Letter for All-Star Status

YOU JUST MOVED UP IN MY MVP PROGRAM TO ALL-STAR STATUS!

To show some appreciation on my end, enclosed is your preloaded All-Star Starbucks card! If you don't want this to be a one-time ten-dollar shot, please leave the card as is and do not transfer it to any other Starbucks account. It's almost impossible to reload the card when it's on another account. An additional ten dollars will be loaded onto your card on the first of every month for the next six months. If during these six months, you provide me with a referral, I'll add an ADDITIONAL twenty-five dollars to your All-Star Starbucks card—and I'll add a six-month extension to your rewards program once I meet with your referral. If, after six months, you don't have a chance to offer me any more referrals, your status will return to MVP. To ensure this doesn't happen, just provide me with another referral! Thanks again for your business!

Appendix B: The CliffsNotes' Version of the Instructions

Congratulations! You've been invited to be a part of my MVP program. Why? you ask. Because you have shown me that you are one of **M**y **V**aluable **P**artners! How is this? you're wondering. It's because you've demonstrated that I'm your Realtor of choice, owing to your current or past business and/or referrals, which I've greatly appreciated over the years.

So what is this MVP Program? It's a way for me to shower you all with monthly gift offerings and exclusive offers, invite you to fun, private events, and really show *my* appreciation for your referrals! There are two levels to my MVP Program. In the first level, everyone will receive a monthly e-mail with the "Offer of the Month." If it's something you are interested in receiving, you simply e-mail or call me back to reserve your gift as soon as you can since most often, there will be a limit on how many are available. This is NOT a drawing, and NO, you don't need to get me a referral to claim a gift! In addition, these gifts are ALWAYS FREE to you!

What if you do get me a referral or decide to do business with me as an MVP? Then you shoot up to the MVP All-Star level! As an All-Star, you'll get your own MVP Starbucks card with ten dollars on it. It doesn't stop there! You'll also have ten dollars automatically loaded on your card on the first of every month for six months! The perks keep coming. If I receive another referral during that six months, you get an automatic twenty-five dollars loaded onto your card as a thank-you. Your free coffee (or tea or pastries or gifts) can extend for years, so long as you send me at least one referral every six months. And what if you don't get me another referral in those next six months? Not to worry; you'll still be an MVP and have access to all of the first-level fun! You can always become an All-Star again at any time with a new referral.

What is a referral? you ask. It is NOT me selling anyone a home. It's simply you getting permission from anyone you know who is thinking of buying or selling a home to give me his or her name and number so that I can call that person and set an appointment to meet. It doesn't matter if I get that person under contract, and it doesn't matter if I close the transaction. How easy is that?

For more information, head to http://www.lizkeepsitreal.com/mvp/

About the Author

Who is Liz Johnson? Do you want the fun version or the serious version? Maybe we should do both.

FUN VERSION

Liz Johnson is a Realtor, cop's wife, former cop herself, combat veteran, mother, entrepreneur, amateur chef, wannabe rap-video dancer, shoe addict, Aquarius, animal lover, gay man trapped in a woman's body, Californian transplant, lazy gardener, avid traveler who wants to see the world, wine drinker, and spaz who is independent, tells it like it is, has an eye for great things, likes to make people laugh, has an irrational fear of rodents, and isn't very nurturing but is really fun to be around.

SERIOUS VERSION

Liz Johnson was born an only child in Los Angeles, California, in the early seventies. After high school, Liz took a year to "figure things out" but only figured out that she better leave Los Angeles for her own good. After a short stint of living with family in Israel, she moved back to the United States and joined the Army. After her four years in the Army, Liz settled in the Seattle/Tacoma area and has stayed there ever since. After the Army, Liz became a sheriff's deputy for the local department and worked as a training officer, undercover officer, and fraud detective. Liz quit law enforcement for a career in real estate because government work breeds laziness, and Liz isn't lazy like that. At the time of this publication, Liz has been a Realtor for twelve years and had her first year of selling a hundred homes in a year thanks to this system. She runs a small team that consists of three administrative assistants and one buyer's agent.

Made in the USA
Columbia, SC
14 November 2021

48629651R00035